Count Your Way through Ireland

by Jim Haskins and Kathleen Benson

illustrations by Beth Wright

Carolrhoda Books, Inc./Minneapolis

To Margaret Emily

This book is available in two editions:
Library binding by Carolrhoda Books, Inc.,
 a division of Lerner Publishing Group
Soft cover by First Avenue Editions, 1997,
 an imprint of Lerner Publishing Group
241 First Avenue North
Minneapolis, MN 55401 U.S.A.

Website address: www.lernerbooks.com

LIBRARY OF CONGRESS CATALOGING-IN-PUBLICATION DATA

Haskins, Jim.
    Count your way through Ireland / by Jim Haskins and
Kathleen Benson ; illustrations by Beth Wright.
        p. cm.
    Summary: A counting book that explores the many facets
of Ireland, including its geography, history, culture, and
sports.
    ISBN 0-87614-872-0 (lib. bdg.)
    ISBN 0-87614-974-3 (pbk.)
    1. Ireland—Juvenile literature. 2. Counting—Juvenile
literature. [1. Ireland. 2. Counting.] I. Benson, Kathleen.
II. Wright, Beth, ill. III. Title.
DA906.H37 1996
941.5—dc20   95-4580

Manufactured in the United States of America
3 4 5 6 7 8 – JR – 05 04 03 02 01 00

Introductory Note

Ireland is a small island off the western coast of England. In 1920, it was divided into two parts—Northern Ireland and the land that would be the Republic of Ireland. Northern Ireland is mostly Protestant. The majority of its people are loyal to Great Britain (which is made up of England, Scotland, Wales, and Northern Ireland). The Republic of Ireland, which is mostly Catholic, was once part of Great Britain but declared itself independent in 1949. Most of the Catholics of Northern Ireland resent British influence in their affairs and would like their country to be part of the Republic of Ireland. This book is about both Irelands, because in spite of their important differences, the two parts of Ireland are bonded by a shared history, language, and culture.

Irish Gaelic (GAY-lihk) is the traditional language of Ireland. It nearly died out after British influence, including the English language, spread over Ireland beginning around the year 1200. In the late 1800s, there was a rebirth of interest in Gaelic, as well as in old Irish folklore and other cultural traditions. Although English is now spoken almost exclusively throughout both Irelands, Gaelic is one of the two official languages of the Republic of Ireland. Gaelic has no official pronunciation, so it may be pronounced quite differently in various parts of Ireland.

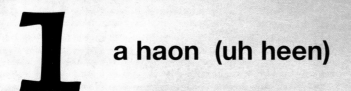

1 a haon (uh heen)

There was **one** Saint Patrick. Although he was not born in Ireland, he is revered as the man who brought the Christian religion to the island.

Patrick was born around A.D. 385 in Scotland. When he was 16, he was kidnapped by Irish raiders and sold into slavery in Ireland. Six years later, Patrick ran away. But he felt a call from God to return to Ireland and bring Christianity to its people. He preached all over the island and became very famous. When Patrick died, around A.D. 460, all of Ireland mourned him.

Many legends have grown up around Saint Patrick's memory. One such legend is that he drove all the snakes from Ireland, which is why there are now no snakes in Ireland. Every year on Saint Patrick's Day, March 17, he is honored not only by the Irish, but also by other people in parts of the world with large Irish populations.

2

a dó (uh doh)

Two structures that mark ancient Irish church settlements are the round tower and the Celtic (KEHL-tihk) cross.

Round towers are five or more stories tall and have cone-shaped roofs. They served as bell towers, lookout platforms, and protection against Viking raiders. The entrances to the towers are about 15 feet above the ground and were reached by ladder. During a raid, the people of a settlement would climb up into a tower and pull the ladder up after them.

The Celtic cross is marked by a round center and short arms and is covered with beautiful carvings. The Celts were a people who came to Ireland from western Europe in about 400 B.C. People consider them to be the original Irish. Traditional Irish art and folk culture is Celtic.

3 a trí (uh chree)

   The flag of the Republic of Ireland has **three** colors: green, white, and orange. The green stands for the Catholics, and the orange represents the Protestants. The white stands for the wish for peace between the Catholics and Protestants, green and orange.

   In the early part of the 20th century, Ireland was to decide whether to remain part of Great Britain. In 1916, Irish rebels captured several government buildings in the city of Dublin. They raised a green, white, and orange flag, which became a symbol of free Ireland.

   Although the British defeated the rebels, the southern part of Ireland eventually won its independence and became the Republic of Ireland. Northern Ireland remained part of Great Britain and continues to fly the British flag.

4 a ceathair (uh kyehr)

Historically, Ireland has been divided into **four** provinces. An old saying describes what each province has been known for in the past:

> Ulster for a soldier,
> Connacht for a thief,
> Munster for learning,
> Leinster for beef.

Ulster is roughly Northern Ireland. Through the years, its geography has helped it resist invasion. The province is surrounded by sea on three sides and humpbacked hills on the fourth. Connacht was once the part of Ireland where people were sent for punishment. Munster contains the cities of Cashel and Cork, where art and learning have long flourished. Leinster's fertile farmland is ideal for raising cattle.

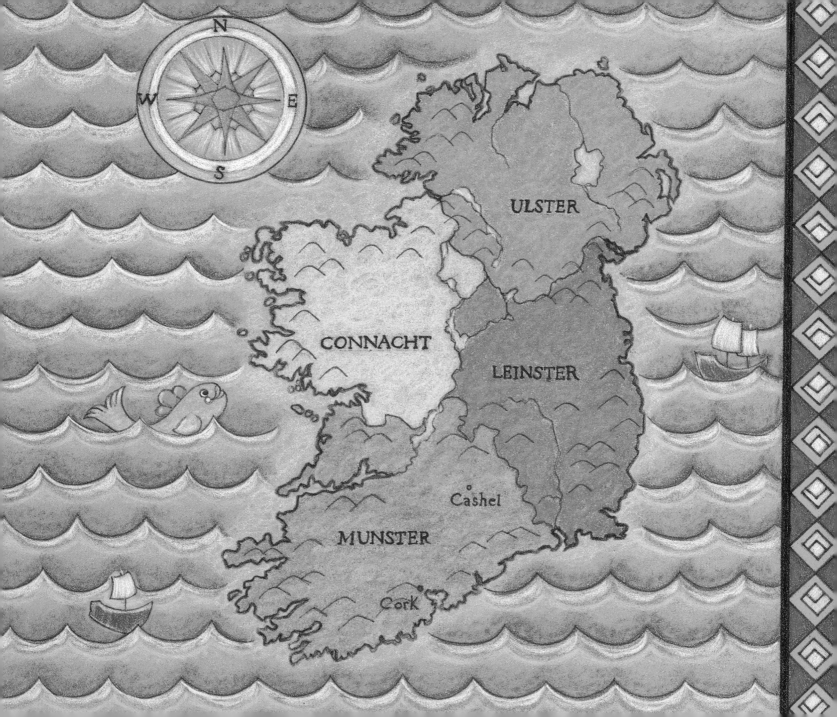

5   a cúig (uh kooihg)

There once was a young woman of Cork
Who needed five baskets of pork.
She went to the town,
Bought pork by the pound,
Then took it all home on a stork.

    There are **five** lines in this limerick. A limerick is a verse of five lines in which the first line rhymes with the second and fifth lines, and the third line rhymes with the fourth. These humorous poems are named after the Irish county and city of Limerick and must have begun there at social gatherings, where a group would sing, "Will you come up to Limerick?" after each set of verses.

    There is a long tradition of poetry in Ireland. Before Ireland had a written language, the history of its people was handed down from generation to generation through poetry.

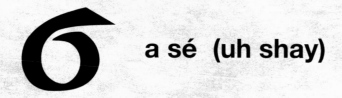

6 a sé (uh shay)

Six symbols of Ireland and Irish culture are the shamrock, harp, *shillelagh* (sheh-LAY-lee), leprechaun, top hat, and clay pipe.

A shamrock is a small three-leafed clover plant. It is strongly associated with Saint Patrick's Day.

The harp is important in many Irish myths and legends. It appears on the national coat of arms and the presidential flag of the Republic of Ireland. The harp is the symbol used to represent Northern Ireland on the royal arms of Great Britain.

A *shillelagh* is a club made from the branch of an oak or blackthorn tree. In early times, an Irishman would use it to defend himself and also to hit the ball in the traditional Irish game of hurling.

A leprechaun is a fairy shoemaker from Irish folklore. His job is to mend the shoes of the other fairies, who spend their time dancing. Perhaps as a result of his hard work, the leprechaun in most stories is rich but also bad tempered.

The top hat and clay pipe are also familiar symbols of the Irish. The "best" clothes of an Irishman once included a hat with a high crown and a narrow brim. At night, once his duties were done and his good clothes put away, a man would sit by his fireplace, smoking a pipe made of the same clay as his cottage.

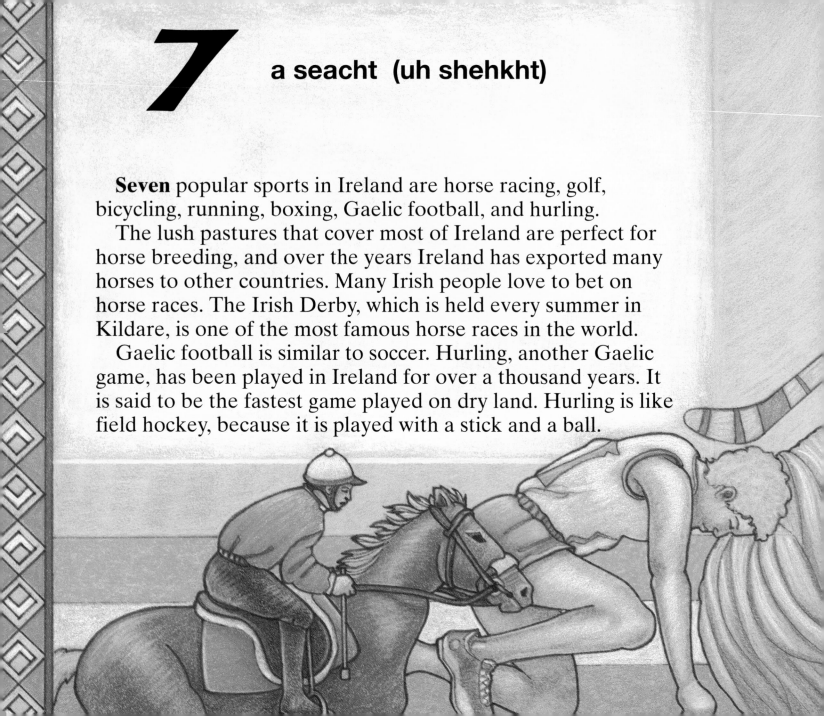

7

a seacht (uh shehkht)

Seven popular sports in Ireland are horse racing, golf, bicycling, running, boxing, Gaelic football, and hurling.

The lush pastures that cover most of Ireland are perfect for horse breeding, and over the years Ireland has exported many horses to other countries. Many Irish people love to bet on horse races. The Irish Derby, which is held every summer in Kildare, is one of the most famous horse races in the world.

Gaelic football is similar to soccer. Hurling, another Gaelic game, has been played in Ireland for over a thousand years. It is said to be the fastest game played on dry land. Hurling is like field hockey, because it is played with a stick and a ball.

8 a hocht (uh hahkht)

Eight traditional Irish foods are potatoes, corned beef, cabbage, mulligan stew, fish chowder, soda bread, oysters, and oatmeal.

Many Irish dishes contain potatoes, which have long been a staple of the Irish diet. Irish cooking also includes a lot of one-pot meals that allow a cook to feed an entire family on only one fish or a bit of meat. Corned beef and cabbage are often simmered with potatoes and served together. Mulligan stew, which is a mixture of whatever meats or vegetables are available, is probably named after a long-ago Irish cook named Mulligan. Most Irish fish chowders contain fish, potatoes, parsnips, carrots, and leeks.

One-pot meals are often accompanied by round, flat loaves of soda bread. Another tasty tradition is a meal of oysters from Galway Bay. Finally, no Irish breakfast would be complete without Irish oatmeal, or porridge.

9 a naoi (uh noyee)

Nine musical instruments important to traditional Irish music are small bagpipes called *uilleann* (IH-lehn) pipes, a drum called a *bodhran* (BAW-rahn), the harp, the tin whistle, the fiddle, the accordion, the wooden flute, the guitar, and the piano.

The revival of interest in the Gaelic language sparked a renewed interest in traditional Irish music, and now there are many festivals of traditional music held throughout Ireland. The music is also played at parties called *ceilidhs* (KAY-lees), where it is accompanied by Irish dances such as reels or jigs.

10 a deich (uh djeh)

Ten handcrafted goods made in Ireland are linen, tweed, woolens, lace, crystal, pottery, china, candles, metalwork, and calligraphy.

The famous Waterford crystal is made in the seaport town of Waterford. The best-known Irish sweaters are knitted in the Aran Islands, located in the deep indentation of Galway Bay on the western coast of Ireland.

Irish lace is famous throughout the world for its intricate designs. Irish calligraphy is also known for its intricacy, and is a tradition that dates back to the time of the Celts.

Pronunciation Guide

1 / **a haon** / (uh heen)

2 / **a dó** / (uh doh)

3 / **a trí** / (uh chree)

4 / **a ceathair** / (uh kyehr)

5 / **a cúig** / (uh kooihg)

6 / **a sé** / (uh shay)

7 / **a seacht** / (uh shehkht)

8 / **a hocht** / (uh hahkht)

9 / **a naoi** / (uh noyee)

10 / **a deich** / (uh djeh)